THE GRINGO GUIDE TO PANAMA

What to Know Before You Go

Elizabeth Vance

THE GRINGO GUIDE TO PANAMA

What to Know Before You Go

DEDICATION

Dedicated to my fellow adventurer-husband and our daughters, who've lived and experienced each step of this amazing journey with me. If it weren't for their support, love and laughter, all of us would have turned tail and left in the first few days after we'd landed.

Also dedicated to my fellow Gringos who are doing their research about a potential move, or are already in Panama and trying to make some sense out of life in this banana republic.

PREFACE

The things I wish someone had told me when (or before) I moved to Panama

You know, it's funny. There are never enough resources to fully prepare you for moving to a foreign country. I'm fortunate to have been in Panama for close to five years. I've read most of the guides that can now be purchased in book or pamphlet form, and there's some critical advice missing about cultural nuances, what you can expect to experience, and how to manage your own expectations for your own happiness. This is especially true for gringos (the common slang name for those of us from North America and Europe), and specifically for those coming from the United States.

So, I've taken it upon myself to put this librito (little book) together. It's something that I wish someone had been kind and straight-forward enough to share with me when we first arrived. Unfortunately I did not have the benefit of that. But that's the reason I've written it. I've heard from many, many gringos who've moved here and struggled because they did not get realistic advice. And many of them end up leaving or feeling disappointed with their move to Panama.

It doesn't have to be that way. Panama is an amazing place, and there's much to be achieved and enjoyed here. But it's also not like anywhere else you've come from.

I hope these thoughts will give you a realistic idea of what moving to Panama as a gringo is really like, and what you can expect to experience. Hold on to your hats, because this ride is not for the faint of heart!

Good luck.

CONTENTS

1

YOU MAY NOT MAKE IT

Life is a challenge; meet it. —Mother Teresa

THE REALITY IS such, that when you move to Panama as a gringo, you really have no idea what you're getting into. I don't say that in a bad way, or to scare you, but it's the truth. You arrive believing it will take you and your family anywhere from three months to a year to acclimate to your new Panamanian life. If you are really optimistic, you think it's going to be less. Because, after all, you're a gringo, and the fact that you chose to leave your country of origin and visit - much less move to – a foreign country, means that you're already an adventurer. You're bold. You believe that you have a great opportunity. Or you came to escape. Whatever. Either way, no matter what the specifics, statistically speaking, you're in the company of less than 2% of all Americans (According to stats listed on MissMoveAbroad.com in 2009).

So you're optimistic. Okay, that's not a bad thing. In fact, in terms of survival and resilience, that's a necessity. The question is how long will your positive attitude last? Only you know the answer to that question, because only you truly know yourself. I cannot tell you what that time period will end up to be. What I'm trying to say here is that Resilience is really the most valuable trait you can have for starting this crazy endeavor called life in Panama.

How is resilience defined? According to Dictionary.com, resilience is a noun, and it means:

> *The power or ability to return to the original form, position, etc., after being bent, compressed, or stressed; elasticity. OR, ability to recover readily from illness, depression, adversity, or the like; buoyancy.'*

This is the perfect word for what you are going to need in the coming days, weeks and months as you move and acclimate to this beautiful country. It's ideal. Why? Because what you are going to experience, in a variety of ways, every single day you are here – whether in the Interior (rural areas) or in metropolitan Panama City – is going to test you, and stretch you beyond the imagination of what you ever thought you could stand.

You're going to get so irritated by the little tiny things that are so different here – in the culture, in the language, in the day to day operations of business, and in the way things happen – that you will, at one time or another:

Want to run screaming back to the airport to leave the country forever,

1. Scream at the top of your lungs at the Panamanian individual with which you are speaking,

2. Throw something (or someone) down to the ground in immense frustration,

3. Board yourself up in your home and never go out again, or

4. Become a really negative person who always slams Panamanians when speaking to other expats, every chance you get.

Now, after reading this list, I feel certain you are thinking, 'Oh my God! This author is evidently extremely negative or jaded or something. I would NEVER do any of those things. I am one of those people who can get through anything.'

You can't hear me, but I'm laughing at that sentiment; because that's exactly what I would have thought five years ago before I moved here. Because I am, like you, a gringo – and I thought, in my gringo/North American/take the world by the tail type of way – that I could overcome anything; that I was different, and that I would do it all with a smile.

Guess what? It took me two full years of being here – on the ground – before I didn't want to run screaming to the airport and return home to the U.S. every single day. And I'm a super positive, super enthusiastic, super handle-everything, go get 'em kind of person. But that's the truth.

I don't know why it is, but the reality is that it takes 99% of gringo expats between 18 months and two full years to acclimate to life in Panama. And that will apply to you, too - no matter where you come from, no matter where you choose to live in Panama, no matter what you do for a living – whether you are retired or working, whether you're married or single, and no matter your race or religion. If you are a gringo and you move to Panama, it will take you this amount of time to acclimate fully.

Does that mean you're going to be miserable during the ac-climation period? No! In fact, you're going to have a normal life, and you're going to find fun, joy and friendship along the way. But this journey WAS a big change for every single gringo I've met here in the past five years, so it's safe to assume it will be for you too.

And by the way, during this time period, I highly rec-ommend you print out a big poster-sized copy of the word Resilience and its definition, and put it everywhere you can in your home so that you see it every day. You might even consider tattooing it on your forehead. Yep, you're going to need to be reminded of how important resilience is – that often.

The Two Year Window

Most gringos who move to Panama don't last more than two years. Many of them return to the USA or go somewhere else much earlier than that, because they have such a hard time getting acclimated. It's important that you realize and get comfortable with the fact that it IS going to take that long to find your way in this country. In Alcoholics Anonymous, the first rule is 'Admit that you have a problem'. It's like that with moving to Panama. If you know upfront that it's going to take two years for you to get acclimated, then you'll be much nicer to yourself along the way. You'll manage your expectations. People who don't manage their own expectations are the ones who end up leaving.

I'll never forget – we had been in Panama for about six months. I was suffering from major depression because I had had a lot of misconceptions about our new life in Panama, absolutely none of which had turned out to be true. So, I was more than a little blue. I went to lunch with a new friend, an expat who had been in Panama for 13 years. My friend could see that I was struggling, and she told me this truth: 'Look, it took me two years to figure it out. That's just what it takes.'

I didn't believe her. I did my usual gringo thing – even in the midst of my frustration. I continued to hold on to the idea that I was different from everyone else. 'That may be the case for you,' I thought. 'But I'll be damned if it's going to take me that long.'

Guess what? She was right.

It's important that you be realistic with yourself and your own process of getting to know and love the country. This book is meant to help you, so that you do find your way here instead of believing a lot of hype that you'll read in other places.

Panama is not the easiest move you'll ever make. So, now that you know that, you can make plans to enjoy the ride. Once you acclimate to Panama, it's a unique and beautiful adventure. But until you get fully broken in, you're going to have some ups and downs getting there.

Fasten your seatbelt!

2

GETTING BEYOND THE GLITZ

*Survivor Panama sign in the Caribbean on
Isla Bastimento, Bocas del Toro*

*"There's a side to you that I never knew, never
knew...." —Adele (Set Fire to the Rain, 21)*

OKAY, TAKE A breath. Now that you know it's going
to be a long acclimation process, you can relax and
have some fun. Be proud of the fact that you're
taking the time to read a book written by someone who's
been exactly where you are. Best of all, besides good advice,
I'm not trying to sell you anything. Not real estate, not a load
of crap, not a seminar to come see the country, not tourism.

7

I've been there, done that. I survived. Better than that, I'm thriving – and, if I did it, you can too.

Maybe you'll remember the phrase, *'Pay no attention to the man behind the curtain'*, from the movie *The Wizard of Oz*? I always laugh when I hear that, because it usually means that's *exactly* what you *should* do: pay attention! Sometimes it means someone's trying to get something by you... take advantage of you, or fool you. Well, it's a good rule of thumb for being a new expat in Panama too. **You've got to pay attention.** Don't assume that the first thing you see or experience is the whole package. It never is.

The first time I saw a picture of Panama City, I was shocked. Shocked, because I had never imagined in my wildest dreams that this city would look so....well...civilized. And not just civilized, but metropolitan, urban, modern, new – but it looks exactly that way. All of those things.

Downtown Panama City from the Cinta Costera

There was a building boom in Panama from 2000 to 2010, especially when it came to high rise buildings in downtown Panama City. A lot of foreign investors bought both commercial and residential real estate (mostly residential) and as a result, a lot of new 30 to 70 story buildings were constructed.

In most U.S. cities, when you see that many skyscrapers in a downtown area, you assume the bulk of them to be commercial office buildings (except for Miami, perhaps). Thus, there's a frequent correlation made – Panama is very often referred to as the Miami of Latin America.

The skyline of Panama City is pretty and has some decent architecture. In fact, with the new Hard Rock Hotel, Revolution Tower, Global Bank Tower, Tower Bank, Trump Hotel, Le Meridian Hotel, the Riu Hotel, and the new Hilton, it's come a long way in just the past five years (since 2007) in that vein.

In fact, the majority of Panama's high rise buildings are residential. And a good portion of the units within those buildings – I'd say at least half – are owned by foreign investors. As of this writing – August 2012 - most of those foreign-owned units are unoccupied or have part-time residents in them, which means that when you are outside the downtown area at night, looking back on the city, it looks like Gotham (the city in the Batman movies). Half the buildings are dark, and it looks pretty weird. It's a phenomenon I'd never personally seen before. In the five years we've been here, it hasn't changed.

The Deception of the Facade

Now, when you first move here and experience all the glitz and glamour that can be found in Panama, you'll be very excited by all of it. Your outlook may be *'Hey, I can do this. This is an interesting place. It's colorful, it's fun, and it's tropical. There's a lot happening here.'*

This is a pretty normal reaction when you've eaten at good restaurants, stayed in a nice hotel like the Trump, Le Meridien, Hard Rock or Manrey. You've danced salsa with well-dressed, English-speaking people at a hip bar or two into the wee hours. You've visited Multiplaza or Metro Mall and been impressed with a number of the name brands you can find there....Gap, Banana Republic, Gucci, Victoria's Secret, 9 West, etc.

Hold on to that sentiment for a while. Panama *can* be very fun, and very glamorous. This is especially true when you've freshly arrived, are staying at a nice hotel, and haven't yet begun your day-to-day life. Soon enough, you'll start to glimpse the man behind the curtain, and the realities below the surface will begin to emerge. Once you get a full-on taste of normal life in Panama, you may feel like you've been rudely awakened.

What am I talking about? Who is this *'man behind the curtain'*? Of course, it's not a real person, it's an expression. The *'man'* stands for all the little realities you're going to soon discover that will make you feel like you've moved to Africa, not to the sophisticated urban place you thought you'd found in Panama.

Try getting your cable TV hooked up. It takes, on average, two to three weeks. Open a bank account - that'll be four to eight weeks. Buy a car. Unless you bring cold, hard cash to the table *(and sometimes even if you do)*, you'll be lucky to have keys in your hand within a month. Then, when you have your new car, get your license plates. Difficult. Sign up for new cell phone service - without handing over your firstborn child – good luck. When you finally have that new cell phone and it gets shut off in the first month because they didn't enter your credit card number correctly for your payments, try getting it fixed over the phone. It'll never happen.

'Huh?' You're thinking. *'Is it really that bad? I've read so many other things about how this is the most sophisticated country in Central America...maybe even in Latin America!'*

Well, you may have read that. And it may be true – but that does not mean it's efficient, or easy. In fact, when you have something happen along the way that is efficient or easy, it's a good time to stop and celebrate it. Because, believe me, it's not the norm.

The reality of Panama is that it's like a coconut. It has the glossy sheen of the newly-built, brand-conscious, scotch-drinking, beautiful facade. But when you crack that baby open and try to get some day-to-day business done, it's not only inefficient; it can be downright maddening. (Feel free to go back to chapter one and refer to that list of things you may, at some point, feel like doing when you get frustrated. You may need it.)

So, what are you to do? Lucky for you, I have a few recommendations.

Lower Your Expectations.

Not just about the fact that the roster of services and products available here in Panama are unlikely to be anything like what you had at home. Lower your expectations about everything.

I've found that if I have no expectations about what's going to come out of any given experience here, I'm much happier with the end result. At minimum, I maintain a better sense of humor.

Allow More Time.

Plan for everything you do in Panama, especially when it involves a service of any kind, to take three times longer than it might if you were in the U.S. That's a reality. Then, if it only takes twice as long, you'll be pleasantly surprised, and that will be worth celebrating.

Find Your Own Solutions.

Don't expect anyone else in this country to solve your problem for you. That would involve critical thinking. Panamanians, as a whole, are not critical thinkers. This sounds like a blanket statement, but most of the time it's the truth.

Most Panamanians are not innate problem solvers – that's just the norm. There are a small percentage of upper-class citizens who attended university and/or boarding school outside the country. These individuals often have a different frame of reference, but they are the minority.

The Panamanian education system does not teach critical thinking. Critical thinking is not taught at home either, in this culture. So, it's best to assume – as a rule - that no one else here will A) fully understand your problem, or B) take the initiative to help you solve it.

That responsibility is solely up to you.

When you **stop** expecting others to solve your problem for you, you will have a much better experience. Don't assume anything. Don't think that someone else will fix your problems. You are better off knowing that any solution lies in your own hands.

When I don't depend on someone else, I don't feel let down. Instead, I have a great sense of humor, laughing at whatever little curves come my way instead of getting upset.

What you'll learn is that if someone does take the initiative, hurrah! It will be a fabulous surprise.

It's safe to assume that you're going to have to use your brain to figure out your problem. Then, you can walk the service person (or whoever is helping you) through the exact steps you need them to take in order to get to the end result you're looking for.

Here's an example. We have a wonderful man who works for us, and has for several years. One of his weekly tasks is to wash the car. One week, after he'd been with us for some time, I realized that he had not washed the car that week. I asked him, *'why did you not remind me about the car wash this week?'* His reply was *'Well, it was not on the list.'* Now, in my mind, since he's worked for us for years, and has washed the car every single week, I would think he might have wondered why that task was not on the list for this particular week. But he did not. That thought did not even enter his mind, until I asked him about it.

Here's what I learned from this experience (and many, many others): direct, specific instruction for a task must be stated verbally or written down *every single time* you expect it to be done. If you don't do that, you cannot expect that the task will get accomplished.

In some ironic way, this is an example of the local culture training you to ask for what you need!

Productivity and the Lack Thereof

Don't compare productivity in Panama to be the same as productivity elsewhere in the world. Because it's definitely not. Panama is, in fact, very unproductive generally. It's an interesting mix of Latin and Caribbean work ethics. You'll find that the locals take the definition of manana (which is Spanish for 'tomorrow') and stretch it out to mean *I'll get back to you when I'm ready*.

Here's food for thought. Panama was occupied (or the battleground of some war or another) for hundreds of years before it became its own sovereign nation in 1903. For many years, Panama was part of Colombia. So, the mindset of the natives for all of those years was one of an enslaved or conquered people. Free thinking was not encouraged or rewarded.

After the country's independence in 1903, the ruling powers kept things pretty much the same (in terms of mindset) until about 20 years ago. The indigenous class was kept on one level, while the educated class tended to rule. This tiny upper class had all the power and control, and they liked it that way. So, as in earlier years of their history, lower class people weren't taught or encouraged to think for themselves. In fact, if they did, they were likely punished (at least in the years before Panama became a democratic republic).

The point is that the mindset (for most people here) is to do only what they are told. That can take a long time for expats to figure out, because most developed nations don't think that way. The purveying lack of productivity can be incredibly bewildering and frustrating.

If you become annoyed (when you're thinking like a gringo), because you're experiencing this non-critical thinking mindset, it's important to know that your success lies in your own hands. Meaning that how you react or respond to someone who is not thinking like you will determine the outcome of the situation. If you get upset or angry, it can lead to major miscommunication. Often, it leads to disaster (or at least a lot of chaos in between). The key to getting what you want is to be very clear in how you communicate, and to drop all of your assumptions about how well anyone understands you, or how they will act.

When you realize this IS the cultural mindset, you can adapt to it. That's right, I said *YOU* can adapt. Because that is what will have to happen if you want to figure out how to thrive here.

It's important to note that if you take the typical gringo approach when you get upset of raising your voice, or yelling, you will be the loser. Panamanians shut down when you yell or your voice escalates, and then things only get worse. So, don't do it. Keep your cool, and you'll eventually end up getting what you need.

Enjoy Your Surprises

You've read it a few times in the paragraphs above. But, I'll say it again, because it's important. *Be surprised* when something happens right the first time. In fact, celebrate it! It's not the way things usually happen here. The little things that *do* go right are worth celebrating, because they don't happen often. Savoring the successful moments will often make up for all of those that seem like they're never going to get finished.

Sometimes it's the little things that keep you going. So, treat yourself to an ice cream cone, or a glass of wine, or whatever little thing that helps you stop and smell the roses. It's part of you maintaining your sanity, especially early on in your acclimation period. And believe me, you will deserve it!

This is Panama (T.I.P.)

Remember, Panama is a *developing* nation. Many people call it a third world country (which technically it is not if you look up that definition in Wikipedia). These realities are part of the way things function here, and they're part of how it is. *You're* the one who chose to move to Panama, so *you're* the one who has to acclimate. You can, you will, and you can have fun along the way.

This is Panama. (Eventually, you'll come to know this phrase as 'T.I.P.' and you'll laugh when you hear it.)

3

Can I Get By With Just My English?

Life's hard. It's even harder when you're stupid. - John Wayne

YOU MAY HAVE read that you can get by in Panama without speaking any Spanish. Is that really true? In short, the answer to this question is a big fat NO. You can't. While 14% of Panamanians speak English as a second language, and that makes Panama the country with the highest percentage of English speakers in Central America, it still means that 86% of nationals do NOT speak English.

So, 8.5 out of 10 times when you are speaking English to someone in Panama, they aren't going to have a clue what you are saying. Get used to it. The general population does not speak English, did not learn it in school, and probably will never learn it. On the flip side, if they do speak English, they'll likely want to practice with you, which can be fun.

In my opinion, I don't think you'll be happy living here if you don't learn any conversational Spanish.

Now, if you're a highly paid executive working only with other international firms, then perhaps you'll be okay and you can function. But, if you plan to do such mundane things as shop at the supermarket, talk to someone about your electric bill, go get your hair cut or take your dog to the vet and don't have *any* Spanish in your vocabulary, you're going to have a hard time. At a minimum, you'll find yourself feeling very isolated. And you will lose opportunities to connect with others in your new country, and that would be a real shame.

Bottom line: Take some classes. It's so affordable. You can have a private tutor come into your home for two hours a week for around $20 a session. It's worth it. And even if it takes you some time, Panamanians are glad to hear you try to speak Spanish, everywhere you go. Don't be embarrassed – just make an attempt. If you prefer online or at-home learning, you can purchase language software and study at your own pace. The key is to commit yourself to studying, two to three times a week, for at least 30 minutes each time.

Is it easy? No. Will it be painful? Probably. But will you feel like you fit in? Will you feel more comfortable in Panama? Will you feel freer if you speak some of the local lingo? Yes.

So just do it. You'll be glad you did.

4

IT'S NOT WHAT YOU KNOW

It's all about who you know

Wise men speak because they have something to say;
Fools because they have to say something. - Plato

Y OU'VE HEARD IT said: It's not what you know; it's who you know. In Panama, that reality is truer - ten times over - than it is in other places.

Often when you meet someone for the first time, the first question they'll usually ask you is: *'What do you do?'*

Well, in Panama, the first question you'll be asked is usually: *'Are you related to...?'*

When someone else's name comes up in conversation, the other person will ask, *'And, are they related to…?'*

Note: In the first year or two after you relocate, if it's obvious that you're a foreigner, the first question may be: *Where are you from?* This may precede the *'Are you related to…?'* query at first. As your Spanish improves, the *'Where are you from?'* question will eventually be dropped.

The intention of these direct questions is to establish who you are, as it relates to the speaker. It lets them know right off the bat where you fall in terms of class, race, social standing and possibly even religion. (For more on this, see Chapter 11.)

That said, it's a real surprise for most expats when they encounter it. Many find it insulting, and feel that they're being asked to prove their bona fides from the very first moment of meeting a person. In fact, that's exactly what it's meant to do, but the practice is Panama is a routine one, and it's not considered rude.

The reality is that Panama is a tiny, tiny place. In the 2011 census, there were 3.3 million people counted on the Isthmus. Of those, 1.1 million were living in Panama City. The upper class comprises the top 1% of the population. That means that this upper-class segment (who influences the country in terms of government and business) totals approximately 33,000 people.

Members of Panama's upper class are active and connected in business and social realms. They are the same people you'll see photographed in the local newspapers and magazines. These are the people you will get to know by first name within one to three years of your move here, especially if are engaged in some kind of business in the country. Most expats that move to Panama are considered to fall into either Upper-Middle class or Upper class, due to their financial standing (compared with the rest of the country).

Now, if you've come from a small place, or grown up in a small town, this fish pond syndrome won't be a big change for you. Because that's exactly what it's like to live in Panama. Everyone knows everyone. That's why those questions – *Who are you?* And *who are they?* – are the norm. You will soon discover that everyone you know is somehow connected to everyone else you know. And it won't just be a feeling – it's true. The spider web of interrelationships in the country can be overwhelming.

Nepotism

In the U.S. and in many other countries, nepotism is frowned upon in the workplace, unless it's a family-owned business. When a family member is hired within a company, the relative is often perceived by others to be treated better or differently and to receive better opportunities. Whether the advantage is real or not can cause a lot of problems within company ranks and even in the company's public perception. That's one reason nepotism is not common in the U.S. Panama seemingly has no problems with nepotism. Nepotism not only happens here; it's smiled upon and it's normal.

That's right. You can expect that Panamanians would *prefer* to hire their family members, or their friends' family members before they'll hire you, because that's the norm.

It's the embodiment of the phrase, *'I prefer to dance with the devil I know than with the friend I don't.'* If there's a choice between a family member and an unknown person, you'll see the family member getting hired. This practice is just a piece of *'who you know'*.

Another reality– and this one is relevant for anyone considering opening a business here – is that if the locals don't know you, they will not work with you. They won't hire you, and they won't buy your products. Thus, it will take you a very long time to build up your business. An integral key to success in business in Panama is the fact that you MUST ingratiate yourself into the local business climate.

To be successful in this market, it's necessary to move in, open your business, start networking, build relationships, prove yourself trustworthy and give it several years. That's right. I said years, not months. Because that's what it takes.

Panamanians are very loyal to other Panamanians. And who can blame them? This is a tiny country. If there weren't some loyalty, most of them would have been out of business long ago. So, in many ways, it's a nice thing. Does it make it fair? Well, no, but so what? It's their country and that's the way it works.

There are a lot of foreign business people finding their way to Panama in recent months and years. Usually they've seen the latest New York Times or Wall Street Journal article touting the strength of Panama's economy. They've read that unlimited opportunity abounds in Panama, and like the gold diggers of generations past, they come to stake their piece of the pie.

Unfortunately, there's a huge misunderstanding (on their part) that *their* business will thrive here just because opportunity exists. They mistakenly think when they arrive, that things will get up and running as quickly and smoothly as they might in their home country. When they don't find immediate success, they lament to everyone they meet (after a month or two) that they're not making inroads here fast enough.

That's just not the way it works here. Your tried-and-true methods for success that you've brought with you from somewhere else simply don't work in Panama. Many business people launch their products and services in this market, thinking they'll be recognized for whatever they're bringing, because it's new, different, or simply new to this market. Unfortunately, the fact that something sells elsewhere doesn't mean it's going to sell in this market. This is a unique, interesting place, and there's no one clear road map for how things function.

The key to success here as a businessperson is to establish yourself. Establish your name, and pay your dues. Invest your time and your money into making the rounds, and getting yourself known. Get serious, make a real investment, and hang a shingle out before you expect any real results.

By the way, you'll be much more successful – faster – if you make a full-time commitment to this market. That means, move here and then establish your business. The back and forth part-year living here and trying to establish a business does not work. The local market wants to know that you're *fully* invested – meaning you are here full-time - before they invest in you. If you're not fully available to them – living in Panama every day - then don't expect them to establish their loyalty with you either.

The key to success in business in Panama is to understand that it doesn't matter how much you know anywhere else. When you come to Panama, you have to get the lay of the land, socially and in business. You have to figure out who's who and how it works, and the earlier you do this, the better off you'll be.

Reminder: This process takes time. Be patient. Have some fun with it. Because T.I.P.

Are you smiling yet?

5
LEAVE YOUR WHITE HORSE AT HOME

There is nothing either good or bad, but thinking makes it so.
- William Shakespeare, Hamlet

THIS CHAPTER IS a segway from the last one, and it's about expectations – again. This is a recurring theme in this book, because your expectations (and how you manage them) are one of the keys to your success in getting beyond your first two years in Panama with flying colors.

When we first came to this country, we had this idea that we were coming in with all our know-how, knowledge and sophistication, and that those things were going to make a difference.

What kind of difference? Well, we weren't quite sure. In my mind, I envisioned that it would be big. I felt that because we'd made the adventurous decision to move our lives here, we were guaranteed a huge accomplishment in the long run.

In past lives, my husband and I had both enjoyed solid professional success. We were proud of that. So we felt like we were bringing a good skill set to the table in this country.

A good portion of why we moved here was for adventure. And the experience has definitely been that, but not necessarily in all the glowing, fun terms we'd previously thought.

Adventure, in the real world, often means there are times that will make you want to scream: sometimes with delight but just as often from fright. And, there will be some downright nail-biting moments along your journey, whether you're looking for them or not.

Somehow, when we came, we thought we were riding in on a white horse (figuratively, of course) to save the day. We were bringing *fresh* ideas, after all. A global mindset. A new perspective. We felt like no matter what we did here, it would be good. Because of the lack of sophistication in the local market, we assumed the simplest idea would be embraced and accepted.

Now, we look back and laugh at ourselves. For a whole lot of reasons, but mostly because of the fact that we had once thought that things here, at *any* point would be (a) simple, (b) accepted, and (c) embraced. We were very naïve.

Well, guess what? There's been plenty of humble pie to go around since we moved to Panama. And most of the time, it's been deserved. I personally had to get over my own attitude – my aggressive American mindset - in thinking I was *just all that*, and that I could make *that* much of an impact in this country and *that* much of a difference. Because guess what? I was wrong.

Do I make a difference? Yes. But it is at the level I previously thought I might? No. Was that a let-down for me? Yes. Was it humbling? Yes. Was it discouraging? Yes. Is this thought process a normal one for many expats that come here? Yes.

Here's the beauty of what we have learned, however. We call it the *Eight Degrees of Difference*. (That's because Panama City is located at eight degrees latitude north of the equator, and 80 degrees west.)

Instead of expecting that any impact we make will be broad, wide, and far-reaching, we now know that the difference we're making in Panama is with the individuals with whom we interact every day. The ones we see and get to know every week – at home, in our daily round, and at work. We're making a difference to them by the way we live our lives. It's so easy to get frustrated when the day-to-day round is slow. Or to get annoyed when your country mates don't think like you do. Or to wonder how many times you have to reiterate the same thing over and over and over at work, before someone *gets* it. It's easy to get discouraged when you feel like your voice is heard, but not listened to. Life in Panama, especially in business, can often feel like you are beating your head against a wall.

These types of differences we may or may not make in Panama are not the ones we thought they might be. The images of Magellan and Balboa discovering the oceans, and bringing newfound innovations to this world have been left far behind. Truly, the impacts we'll make may be small. They may never be recognized, but we know they're there.

The giving up of your own ideals of *What this Panama Experience Will Be* is something we've had to come to grips with. What we thought and what it really is – well, those are two very different things. A big part of my own misconception was that I expected to be recognized, accepted, and embraced in this culture – as a person or because of my ideas. I was wrong, and my misconception led to me being disappointed. Very little of what I thought would happen did happen. It was more of an ego trip, to be honest.

What I'm saying is that your own experience in this country lies in your hands. Don't come with unrealistic ideas or visions of grandeur. Don't expect that because you were accepted or acknowledged elsewhere that you will be here. Don't think that any change you will introduce will be welcome. The only person you'll disappoint with these types of expectations is you.

Instead, when you have no (or at least, reasonable) expectations of what will come to you on your journey here, or in what way you will *really* be able to contribute to life in Panama, guess what? Every single thing you can or do achieve in your new life in Panama will become a pleasant surprise, and perhaps a personal treasure.

6

The Friends You'll Make ... and Those You Won't

Friendship is born at that moment when one person says to an-
other: What! You too? I thought I was the only one. - C.S. Lewis

ANOTHER OF MY big ideas was that we would make lots of new Panamanian friends. I don't know why we specifically assumed they would all be national citizens – Panamanians – but we did.

Well, guess what? In the first 18 months of living in Panama, we had exactly one friend who happened to be Panamanian. Let me define what I mean by *friend*.

First, when I use the word *friend*, I'm not talking about the people you work with every day in your office. Those are colleagues, and you may get along just fine with those people. In fact, normally, that's the case.

We've found, in a business setting, that Panamanians are absolutely warm, welcoming individuals. But let's establish that the true friendships I am talking about here are those you have outside the workplace. Or outside your child's school contacts, if those only exist within the framework of school activities.

We had really hoped to make some friendships in those early months and years with some of the locals. We envisioned barbeques and beach outings and dinners out with fellow spouses and so forth. But those relationships never materialized (except for the one friend previously mentioned).

In any case, if you share or have this vision of developing new friendships with Panamanians, then please be advised that it is, in fact, pretty unlikely that you'll find those, at least at first.

Originally, I was actually offended. In fact, I took it very personally. I got mad. Then, I was hurt. Then, I turned the anger back at myself: *'what is wrong with me/us that the locals don't want to socialize with us?'*

Of course, this thought process did not make me feel more positive about our move to Panama. In fact, it made me feel pretty depressed.

So, why weren't we connecting with the locals? Let me explain.

First, we have to go back to the family make-up of Latin Americans. Unlike us folk from many other places (and especially the U.S.), families in Latin America actually stay close to one another. Both physically (as in proximity) and emotionally.

They don't move away from each other and separate like we do in the U.S. In fact, in most Panamanian families, young single people – even into their 30s - continue to live in the family home with their parents until they marry.

You may laugh, but this is the truth. It's the norm here. Plus it's cheaper (at least for the younger generations).

Second, when grandparents are older, they often move in with their children. Then, suddenly, you have a large family home that includes three generations – the parents, grandparents and children.

So, when family gatherings or get-togethers materialize here in Panama, they include not only these three generations, but any extended family members brought into the family by marriage. So, that includes the in-laws, children, cousins, nieces, nephews, aunts, uncles, brothers, etc. etc. etc. Including those once, twice and sometimes three times removed!

The bottom line is that a typical Panamanian family is 50 to 400 persons strong when you count up all of these individuals. And not only family members keep in touch with each other *daily* – they get together *every weekend*! Maybe not every single person is involved every single weekend, but a good portion of them will have some type of a family-related event each and every weekend of the year.

Think of it. When you consider 300 people in a year with 365 days and include birthdays, christenings, baptisms, weddings, reunions, suddenly you realize that Panamanians' social calendars are pretty full, just with their family commitments.

So, the bottom line here is that most Panamanians are simply too busy to socialize with you. Culturally, they are taking care of their own.

If you feel slighted in the least by this practice, please don't. The family nucleus is so close and so tight here in Panama, that if one member chooses not to attend a family event, they'll pay for it! They'll get phone calls, emails, texts, and questions from everyone else that did attend... if they don't show up and participate.

Once I understood how family systems function here, I no longer took it personally that we did not have many Panamanian friends. Instead, I realized how complicated it can be for them. Part of me thought *'How Cool! Wouldn't it be great to have a family that big, and to actually be close to them?'* The other thought was *'No way! I don't want to feel obligated to that many people, that often, no matter how much I love them.'*

So, you see the family structures locally have their positives and negatives, and really have nothing to do with you and me.

The good news is that if and when you make a real friend with a Panamanian, you will know for certain that it is a real friendship.

Yes, these friendships take longer to materialize. But you can take stock that when it happens, you will truly have that friend for a long time, if not for life.

So, who *will* you make friends with once you move here? Easy. There are lots of other foreigners who have come to live in Panama – either for work, to retire or to be here part-time. There's your pool of new friends and social contacts. You will naturally have an automatic connection with most other expats here. Because you are one yourself!

Consider this. We have been here five years. Our best friends in the first two years were from Sweden. While these friends moved after a few years, we've been fortunate to maintain our friendship with them across the ocean. Now our closest friends are from Colombia. We're also fortunate to have many friends from a plethora of other countries: Canada, other U.S. citizens, Venezuela, the U.K., Mexico, Chile, Uruguay, China, and the list goes on. Panama is kind of like an Ellis Island – it's a melting pot of expats from around the globe.

Who knew? And where else in the world can you have such a cross-cultural experience, just because you all end up in the same place? So, there's hope for you, my friend. You'll find that most expats, no matter where they hail from originally, love to meet and greet here, because we're all foreigners. And, as such, we're sharing this crazy life experience that can only be known as T.I.P. We feel so fortunate to enjoy so many interesting friendships that we *never* would have made, if we had not come to Panama. You'll discover the same.

Places to Go

Here are some recommendations of where to go to meet other expats. The Balboa Yacht Club, a Cheers-like atmosphere with great burgers and cold beer in Amador, is one such place. Rincon Suisse Restaurant is another in El Cangrejo. There are countless others. Pick up a copy of the local English newspaper, aptly named *The Visitor*, and you'll find a calendar of events, as well as lot of ads for places where English is widely spoken.

Balboa Yacht Club - a popular gathering place for expats in Panama

Good luck and congratulations! The most rewarding experiences for us have been the new friendships we've made. And, while it did take longer to form friendships with some of our Panamanian friends, we now count many of them as friends too. (We don't see them as frequently, but when we do, we really enjoy them.) This is the beginning of a new chapter for you and your life in Panama.

7

IT'S CHEAP TO LIVE HERE...MAYBE

THERE'S NOTHING THAT annoys me more than promotional groups that market Panama with campaigns that insinuate one can live on less than $800 a month in this country. This claim should be equated with those bait and switch campaigns that were the norm on late night television in the 1980's.

Come in and buy this TV for just $199. But when you get there, and look for that particular television set, oops! The sales person tells you they just sold the last one, but they happen to have another one that's just a tad more expensive (with more options, more whatever, etc. etc. etc.).

Here's the truth. Anyone who tells you that it's possible to live for $800 a month in Panama is selling you a bill of goods. Because you will be living far away from civilization in a little town, away from anything convenient and certainly not on the beach. You won't be close to most places where you really might like to be if you're going to move across the world to be somewhere cheaper.

Now, if your only reason for choosing this country is to lower your costs, then it's very possible that Panama is the place for you. But, if you are looking for something for nothing, then I suggest you look elsewhere. (Unless of course something located in the middle of nowhere is exactly what you had in mind. And if so, good luck to you. But, please move there knowing that there certainly won't be any other Gringos there, except maybe a few hiding from the law.)

Here's the reality. If you live anywhere in and around Panama City, in a nice condo or apartment which has any level of standard first-world construction (or close to it), you're going to pay *equal or similar rent or purchase prices* as those you would expect to find in many cities in the U.S.

Equivalent cities might be Houston, or Cleveland, or Phoenix. If you're coming from Manhattan or San Francisco, then of course, you'll find places much less expensive in Panama City. But most people who relocate from the U.S. discover that Panama is not nearly as inexpensive as they were led to believe.

Is Anything Less Expensive in Panama?

Here's what you can realistically expect to cost less, the same, or more if you are comparing it to a place like... I don't know... let's use Austin, Texas, as an example.

Real Estate – Buying Or Renting
A Place To Live

If you live smack downtown in Panama City, you're going to pay high prices. If you want to live where the action is – walking distance to bars, good restaurants, the shopping districts, the higher end neighborhoods, and the two large parks in the city – then you're going to pay for that access.

There's no savings here between what you'd pay in Austin, Texas, versus what you'll pay in Panama City, not really. Not if you get a place that you – as a gringo – would consider really habitable and comfortable.

Downtown Panama City

NOTE: If you're happy living in a *very* simple home with no finishes, then you can find something that will fit the bill. But it won't be in a neighborhood you really want to live. Most gringos seem to want to maintain the same level of quality in their housing as they had in their home country.

In Panama, when you find a place that has a higher level of interior (and certainly exterior) finish, the bottom line is it's a commodity. You can expect to pay more for it. And, as the saying goes, you get what you pay for.

Food

Depending on what you like to eat day to day, you can expect to pay more for some food stuffs and less for others. Our food bill is about the same month to month as what we paid in the U.S. That sounds crazy, but it's true.

Here is a list of things that are generally much less expensive in Panama at the grocery:

- Fresh fish
- Baked items – if they are locally produced
- Locally grown fruit
- Locally grown vegetables
- Chicken
- Pork

The best fruit is often found at a roadside stand

Here are examples of things that are generally more expensive at the grocery:

- Anything made outside the country that must be shipped in – including most of your normal brands for anything boxed, frozen, dried, etc.
- Any of the brands you know and love from the U.S.
- Comfort foods like your favorite peanut butter or popcorn, or anything manufactured.

- Beef. Unless you prefer grass-fed local beef, which most gringos don't. It's tougher, they cut it in different ways than we're used to, and it's pretty bland. Once you get used to it, you may love it. Me? I prefer good old USDA cuts, which means they must be imported and are more expensive.

The bottom line is: you can expect your grocery bill to be *about the same* as what you generally pay in the U.S. I don't care what anyone else says. That's the truth.

Services

A-ha! Now, here's some fantastic news. When it comes to services, because labor is very affordable in Panama, you'll save a lot of money. Here are some examples.

- A haircut at a decent salon costs $8 for men, and $15-20 for women. If you want something higher end, you can find it, but you'll pay more.
- Ladies, for getting your nails done, you can get a mani-pedi for $15 in the salon, and pay $25 for a gal to come to your home and do them.
- Massages run $20-30 per hour. Now, the typical style of massage learned here is generally a bit less sophisticated than other places. It's called Relajante (which means relaxed) and it's a lighter touch than the technique used in a typical Swedish massage in the U.S.
- Taking your pet to the veterinarian costs about ⅓ of what it does in the U.S.

- A full-time maid, five days a week, will cost you $15-25 per day.
- A full-time secretary costs $800 a month. (This does not include social security and other benefits, just straight salary.)
- A doctor's appointment costs $25 to $50.
- X-rays cost $25.
- An overnight hospital stay can be as little as $250.

You get the picture. Here, you can afford a lot of services for a lot less money than you can in other more developed countries. That's nice, and it's easy to get used to. And, frankly, when you're new in the country, you can very likely use a weekly massage to take the edge off of your move, so go ahead and indulge. It might just become a habit!

8

THE GRINGO TAX....
A.K.A. JUEGA VIVO

If you can't do anything about it, laugh like hell. - David Cook

WHEN YOU COME to Panama – whether to visit or to live – and you don't speak Spanish, you can expect to encounter pricing that's about 20-30% higher than what a local might pay. How is this possible? Well, for starters, if the person you're doing business with can see that you don't speak the language, then he has a lot of leeway for not explaining to you why a price might be higher for you than for anyone else. And, usually, bottom line, he or she is taking advantage of you.

Normally, this will happen in a local store where pricing is not marked, or in a local market where you might purchase fish, vegetables, or tourist crafts. It also happens when you buy cars or larger-priced items. It's not as likely to happen in a store at the mall, unless there are no printed prices (though that's pretty unusual). And it happens a lot in taxicabs.

It used to make me mad when this would happen to me. Now, I just laugh. Because I do speak Spanish, so I can usually figure out quickly whether someone is trying to rip me off. (Again, note that some knowledge of the Spanish language is very important.)

Here's what may happen. You pick up an item. You ask for the price. The person assisting can tell you don't speak Spanish (or they may speak to you in limited English). A price is given. Now, because you don't know normal prices in Panama, the price may be acceptable to you. In fact, the price may be about the same or even slightly lower than what you might expect to pay in the U.S. So, you pay it.

You don't know any better. The sales person knows it's a much higher price. So, they keep the profit above the normal cost for themselves. They win, you lose. Locally, this is called *Juega Vivo*, which literally translates to the Game of Life.

When you've lived here for several months, you'll discover that you've paid for things at prices MUCH higher than the norm here. Then, you might get mad. The experience will make you a much better negotiator as time goes on, and as you live here longer. More importantly, as your Spanish language skills improve, you'll also be in much better shape. You'll figure out what things really cost, and how much you should expect to pay for that item or service.

Here's an example. When my husband and I first visited Panama, our hosts asked us not to take a cab on the street. We consider ourselves pretty adventurous, so one afternoon, we took a walk. Then, we got tired because it was so hot. We flagged down a cab. We had the cab take us on a mini-tour around the city for about an hour. We never asked for a price when we got in the cab.

NOTE: Before you *ever* get into a cab in Panama, you should inquire if the driver will take you to your location, or not. If he says yes, you then agree on a price - b*efore* you get into the cab.

Anyway, we didn't know this. So, we got in, took a ride and paid $35. Now, that was in 2007. A $35 fare for an hour ride is unheard of, even today. In mid 2012, that same ride should cost about $20 (back in 2007, it probably should have cost $15). (An exception to this would be if you are catching an airport shuttle, which requires the driver to take you and return to the city.)

The best way to understand this cultural bad habit – *Juega Vivo* – is to realize that the ruling party took advantage of the locals for hundreds of years. History is generally consistent in that when one person rules another, there's not a lot of opportunity for the underdogs.

When you've lived like that for a long time, it becomes a cultural norm. When an opportunity presents itself to get ahead – even at your fellow man's expense – it's probably likely you'll take that opportunity. That's where *Juega Vivo* comes from. It's kind of like the Man from the 1970's – the striking out against the establishment. Not everyone does it. But it happens enough, that it's given Panama a bit of a bad reputation. You're the establishment – or the Gringo – in the minds of those that might try to take advantage of you, so just be aware of it. Many people refer to this as corruption.

Now that we've lived here for several years, I simply smile when someone tries to pull the old *Juega Vivo* price trick. I speak to them in Spanish, I tell them I live in Panama and I will not pay a higher price. This normally cuts the advantage right out of the game!

9

INNOVATION AND EFFICIENCY

Local farmers often bring their wares to the city

Time is an illusion. Lunchtime doubly so.
- Douglas Adams, the Hitchhiker's Guide to the Galaxy

A LOT OF Gringos come to Panama and thumb their noses at the locals. They don't mean to, but that cocky American spirit sometimes comes off that way. In fact, more often than not, it does.

You've heard the term 'ugly American'? Well, we've never met quite as many of them anywhere as we have here in the tiny country of Panama. Often enough, we run into other

Americans in a restaurant, and when they hear us speak English they kind of latch on to us. Next thing we know, they're loudly protesting how horrible the service is, or how they can't find this or that, and how rude Panamanians are. It's embarrassing, and they look like a bunch of jerks. It's amazing how some Americans can so easily forget their manners.

The bottom line is this. You chose (or are choosing) to live in Panama. So, come here with an open mind. Accept the fact that things are different here. This is a developing nation! It's had some American influence over the years, true, but it's not your home country, nor will it ever be. When you have challenges and struggles, deal with your dissatisfaction in the most positive way you can. And, as much as possible, do it with grace and humor. At the very least, be polite. Unless there's a reason to get angry with the locals, it won't do you a whole lot of good.

Nothing is more distasteful than hearing my fellow Americans being loud and rude in a public place with their exclamations about Panama (in Panama). And, trust me, Panamanians take it very personally. (If you thought you were getting bad service before, watch it get worse from that point forward!)

Statistics of Interest

Let's look at some statistics. Less than 20% of U.S. Citizens hold passports, according to a CNNTravel.com (in an article dated February 4, 2011). That's less than half the percentage held by most other first world countries. More significantly, less than 2% of Americans ever choose to live outside the U.S.

Now, with 196 countries around the world to choose from, it's no surprise from the tiny percentage of that 2% of Americans who live outside the U.S. - a microscopic percentage choose to come to Panama. In the group that moves here, you'll encounter everything from soup to nuts.

It's a given that every single expat that moves here is an adventurer in some way. And, while we're all lumped together here, especially for those of us from North America, it's important to be cognizant of getting to know your new neighbors or country mates well before you trust them. I tell you this from experience.

We've met all kinds of interesting individuals that have come to Panama from North America, including:

- Those running from the law.
- People running from the IRS.
- People running from ex-spouses.
- Normal people.
- Law abiding people.
- And some really strange people.

No matter what, you'll encounter an interesting mix.

Whereas in the States, there are an estimated 350 million total population, here in Panama, the U.S. citizen count is maybe 25,000. (Note that this is not an official tabulation; a recent search on the website for the U.S. Embassy in Panama at Panama.usembassy.gov did not yield any official statistics.)

So, the pool of those U.S. citizens whom you will meet here is much smaller, and any craziness that exists will stand out more than it did at your suburban BBQ in Detroit or wherever you hail from.

Anyway, back to that microscopic statistic. Of the miniscule amount of U.S. citizens that choose to move to Panama, everyone comes for different reasons. Some come to retire. Some come to work. Some come for the adventure. Some come so their kids can have a different upbringing. Whatever a person's reason for coming, the point is that you'll meet some really engaging, fun people and you'll also meet some people you probably will want to avoid. So, your social life here will always be both entertaining or interesting, and likely both. But it will never be dull.

Leave the Attitude at Home

Many newly-relocated Americans have a pretty elitist attitude. Normally, it's not that they mean to, they just do. This seems to be a byproduct of people coming here with unrealistic expectations and having those expectations smashed to bits by reality.

How can you avoid this happening to you? First, leave your white horse idealism at home, as outlined in Chapter Five. I cannot count the number of times I've met someone who acts like they are going to save Panama by their presence, because they're bringing X idea, product or service here, that's never been done here before. That the innovation they have the license to is going to make them rich, and that everyone should kiss their feet because they brought it to Panama.

Now, this may be true. You may be bringing something as simple as a new type of product or service to Panama, and that's great. But, leave behind the attitude that everyone here locally should have an instant appreciation for it. Because that's not going to be the case.

Things in this culture have functioned a certain way for a long time, and the system works. I'm not saying it's perfect. It's not. But it works. And, there are reasons it works. I'm not going to go into those here. (That's probably a political-psychographic analysis that would take much longer to research than to write, and that's not up my alley.)

What's important to take away here is this. Don't expect anyone else to care just because you moved to Panama. Because most people don't care.

Moving Here for Business

If you come here for business, awesome. The best advice I can give you to get connected with other professionals and to start networking as soon as you can. Relationships in business in Panama are everything. So, the sooner you start building those relationships, the better off you'll be.

Second, leave your North American expectations of efficiency at home. The relationship building will take a minimum of two full years, if not longer. Why? Because expats have a tendency to come and go from Panama. The average time period for an expat moving into Panama and then moving away again is two years. So, the locals expect that you've come here, you'll be here for two years, and then you'll return to wherever you came from.

When you come here as an entrepreneur, expect that two-year time frame of finding your way in the business

community to be a bit longer, unless you already have con-
tracts in place. If you do, great. If you don't, it's best to have
a back-up plan. Hopefully, you've got some solid savings in
place, to get you through the lean start-up years.

Tips for Success

- *Do what you came to do, and keep doing it. When it gets tough and the results are minimal, keep on doing it. The difference you'll make here in Panama with your work takes a long time to show. Remember the **Eight Degrees of Difference** idea (introduced in Chapter Five)? Take pride and comfort in the fact that you're doing **something**!*

- *Don't look for validation from locals for whatever you're doing. They likely don't get it, or they don't care. If you believe in what you're doing, your own belief will have to buoy you for a while, until your work/business/ideas are embraced and accepted.*

- *Network, network, network. Join the American Chamber of Commerce. Get active with local professionals, both expat and Panamanian. Go down to the Balboa Yacht Club and get to know the local expat characters over a beer. You can swap stories and laugh. Those things will be your best medicine. Locate a variety of social clubs and associations for foreigners, and get involved.*

- *Make some local expat friends, as a support base for yourself. They know what you're going through. They've been there, done that themselves, and it will help you adjust.*

10

LOCAL HABITS, CUSTOMS, COURTESIES AND FORMALITIES

Toucans outside my window

Mind Your Manners
Never miss a good chance to shut up. - Will Rogers

PANAMA IS A huge fish bowl. It's the biggest small town I've ever seen. I grew up in a town of less than 5,000 people in the Southern U.S., where everyone knew everyone and rumors ran rampant. It was a place much like the old TV show *Cheers*: Everyone knew your name. Once

55

you established your reputation, you could never get away from it.

It's the same in Panama. In the business world of Panama, there are about 10,000 executives. That's not many. It's a tiny, tiny pond, so, it's important to watch your step. It's important to know what lies beneath the tranquil surface of this pond, before you put on your bathing suit and dive into the water. Because it's not as simple nor as pretty as it looks.

It's A Small World After All

We've all heard the advice *'You don't get a second chance to make a first impression.'* Keep that phrase in mind. Because when I tell you that everyone here knows everyone, it's absolutely the truth. There may be one level of separation by marriage, but most of the time, the person you just met is related to someone else you work with.

For those that grew up in Panama, imagine how hard this can be: If you were the geeky kid in Math class; if you threw up on your date's dress at the prom; or when your sister had an affair with her boss. Everyone knows your business. Any drama that has ever happened in your life, your entire social circle knows about it. Many of them will never forget those things. It's that small town reality that can make life really tough.

At the same time, there's a lot of comfort and loyalty that comes with this familiarity. Your best friend will literally be your best friend all your life. He'll send you business all your life. Your brother's wife went to school with your third cousin. About 98% of the time, there will be some kind of a connection between you and everyone else that falls into your social circle. That's why the first question you'll be asked when you meet someone for the first time in Panama is *'Are you related to....?'* (This topic was covered at length in Chapter Six.)

Remember the earlier information covered about Latin American connections? With extended families of 300 to 400 people strong, it's hard to break into business here. Why would a local choose you when his mother's first cousin offers the same service? This is the loyalty factor. Everyone knows everyone.

What does that mean for you? DISCRETION is the name of the game. Be the best version of yourself that you can be, and be that consistently. Be forthcoming, straightforward, and honest. Don't be a gossip, not even to your best friend.

Many expats get into the gossip game here. Before you know it, that casual comment you made to your new bridge partner Tuesday night will be front page news at the Who's New lunch by Friday. And, it will likely come back to you with a new twist.

Of course, the natural tendency is to think 'Oh, that won't happen to me.' Everyone thinks that. Then when it does happen, they're incredulous. You can always act surprised when something comes back to you that you originated, with *'No, I hadn't heard that. I had no idea...'* With a sense of humor, this can become unending entertainment. However, it can also be dangerous.

THE GRINGO GUIDE TO PANAMA

Take all of this with a grain of salt. Expect that the gal who is your bank executive is the sister-in-law of the guy you met at the golf club last night. You can bet that he already knows your financial wherewithal, or that he can find it out with a simple phone call. *'What?'* You say, *'Is there no privacy here?'* Did I forget to mention that? The answer is that privacy may exist in theory, but it does not exist in reality. Everyone discusses everything. There are no secrets here. Bad news is sought after like candy, and high drama is considered a prize. Confidential tidbits will often known by everyone in the office by the time the person receiving the information hung up the phone. The concept of appropriateness of discussing someone else's confidential news (like salary levels or bank account balances) has either never been learned in Panama, or it's simply ignored. (*Remember, small town?*)

Panamanians are fiercely loyal to each other. When there's a choice, they'll choose their family and their friends, or even any other national, before they choose you. This applies even when your price is lower, and your service is better. Especially, when it comes to social invitations (as outlined in Chapter Six). Again, it's not personal. That's just the way it is.

Useful Tidbits:

- *Anything you don't want shared with the public at large in Panama should not be spoken out loud in this country. Except maybe to your spouse behind closed doors.*

- *Don't gossip. Anything you have said about anyone in Panama – even in jest – will come back to bite you. Don't let a few cocktails make you think otherwise. You'll regret it.*

Treatment of Women

Panama is in many ways a dichotomy, in the way people are treated. On one hand, the *machismo* in this country can be pretty disheartening, especially for women. On the other hand, women rule the family systems as they age, and the grandmother or mother of the family becomes the family matriarch over time.

Matriarchs are highly revered in this country. In fact, most family gatherings on the weekends are guided by what the ladies want to do.

For that reason, Mother's Day in Panama is a national holiday. The date falls on December 8 each year, and it is considered a national holiday. The date can fall on any day of the week, and the entire country shuts down. Lavish gift giving ensues, as well as the ceremony of pampering Mom in every imaginable way. Mother's Day is absolutely one of the most important family gatherings of the year, and people are religious about it. For church-going families, the holiday starts in church with a morning mass or service.

There's a beauty to this, in that the women of the country seem to gain their power later in life.

Unfortunately, younger women in Panama are often objectified, which is a shame. In every other way, however, equal opportunity does not exist in Panama for women – not in the workplace, and not on the street. From an outsider's perspective, it's very interesting to observe what this looks like – but you'll see it everywhere. For those of us from the U.S., it's like stepping back 30-40 years.

Common courtesy toward women, however, does exist. Men open doors for women. Seats on a bus or in a waiting area are often offered to older women, or women with children, when they arrive. There are reserved parking spaces for pregnant women in front of many businesses. Maternity leave for women in Panama totals three to four months, with time off before and after the baby's arrival. In fact, Panama's labor code requires that if a woman becomes pregnant under your employ, the company is required to maintain her position and pay her for *at least a year* after the birth.

Here are some other courtesies afforded to women that you'll notice here:

- When a woman is being seated (at a restaurant, for example), the waiter often pulls out a chair and assists her in getting seated.
- When a woman enters a meeting, the men will often stand.
- When a woman gets up from her seat in a restaurant (at least in a formal setting), the men at her table will stand. When she returns, they'll do the same. (This has not been common in the U.S. now for some time.)
- Service people commonly greet women callers and visitors with '*Senora*', which is the equivalent of '*Ma'am*' in English. (They use the same title for men – '*Senor*'.)

While these courtesies are prevalent today in Panama, the dichotomy is that a lot of sexual harassment and discrimination also exists. This is a country of seemingly conflicted views on women. For more on that topic, read Chapter Eleven.

Common Courtesy and Cultural Norms

While some of the above courtesies toward women may make you sentimental, you'll notice common courtesies considered standard in other places lacking in a pretty significant way. It's interesting really, but the lack of some of these things will come as a rude awakening. Read more below about a variety of these surprises.

Cell Phone Use

Panamanians love their cell phones. Cell phones are a show of how important you are, in addition to being communication devices. Phone calls are taken no matter what time it is, who they're with, whether or not a meeting is taking place, or how long the phone call goes on. Generally, a full conversation ensues at a normal tone of voice (or a loud one) even if the person receiving the call had been in the midst of a sentence while speaking to you. This, of course, fully interrupts any interaction you were having with that person prior to the ring of their phone.

This can be extremely disconcerting when you are:
- In line at a service counter (and the service person takes the call),
- In a business meeting (and your presenter or colleague takes the call),

- With a friend or colleague enjoying a meal, or
- Any other situation where you've taken the time to have a face-to-face with the other person.

This habit is considered by most foreigners to be extremely annoying and rude. Truth be told, it is both of those things. However, it's the way it is in this country, so you'd better get used to it.

The one thing you can do is to set rules for your own meetings (in your own company, or within your department if you are an executive) about your own employees taking calls. It will be a cultural shock to them, but if you reinforce it consistently, they will eventually adapt.

Personal Space

We're all familiar with the concept of personal space, right? In the U.S., generally you don't get closer than 12 to 24 inches (or more, if you're European) to a colleague or friend when you're standing or sitting side by side, having a conversation. If you are hugging or greeting them, then perhaps you get closer.

Remember the skit about the 'close talker' on Seinfeld a few years back? The guy (or gal) that has no concept of personal space, always gets right in your face, and is so close that you can smell their breath? (And naturally their breath is really bad?)

In Panama, personal space does not exist. At least, it does not exist in the terms you're used to. People in Panama are used to getting close – *very* close – even in a business setting, on a regular basis.

This made me very uncomfortable at first. I felt my space was being invaded. For most expats, this cultural norm is surprising and invasive. It takes some time to get used to it.

Here's what happens. Big families are a norm in Panama, and they don't grow up with much space. Forget the norm of those of us that raised families in the U.S. in the suburbs in sprawling houses. That did not happen here.

Unless you are a member of the upper class (i.e. wealthy) in Panama, you probably grew up in a small apartment or house. It's likely you had a lot of siblings. Many family members sleep together in the same room, maybe even in the same bed. Everyone is crammed together all the time: at church, on the bus, and on the couch trying to watch TV. Everyone grows up used to not having any space to themselves; so the locals are accustomed to being close to one another.

Thus, the concept of personal space does not exist. People stand close to one another - like two or three inches close - or sometimes even touching, when they've never even met.

This is probably one of the most uncomfortable things you need to understand when you move here, and it took me some time. When you come from a culture that values personal space, having someone whisper in your ear, or put their face three inches from yours to tell you something, or stand so close to you that you can feel their body heat can really, *really* irk you.

It's a pet peeve of mine to have someone stand over my shoulder when I am on the computer or looking at something at a desk or table. My Spanish teacher used to do this to me all the time.

Over time, you do get used to it. And it won't bother you, or you just get to where you accept it. In fact, if you live here long enough, the lack of personal space will become your norm, and when you go back to your home country, you'll notice that you keep trying to stand closer to your friends, and they'll keep moving away from you!

It's happened to me several times, before I catch myself doing it. Then, I just have to laugh. Trust me, you will too. But it may take you some time to get there. In the meantime, carry a pack of gum to offer to your close-talking country mates.

Panamanians are used to standing in line

The personal space issue also impacts some other habits locally. These include:

Standing In Line

Panamanians are so used to waiting (remember the topic of efficiency) that they'll stand in line for hours. Sometimes a *line* will not look like the single-file, orderly kind that you might have learned in grade school.

In many experiences, the line turns into a cattle call with people crowding the door and fanning out in all directions. Order does not exist. Nor does the courtesy of a person moving out of your way when they are in your path as you attempt to enter or exit a doorway exist in this country. You will get right up next to someone, and try to pass, and receive a blank stare as if they have no idea what you are trying to do. You'll get used to pushing through, as needed, to get to where you need to go. It's not comfortable, but the subtle hints of indicating to someone with a look or a nod of your head (that you're going in a certain direction and could the other person please move) are generally not understood. So, you have to do what you have to do.

Exiting A Plane

The manner in which Panamanians exit a plane (when coming into Panama or leaving the country at the first stop) is something that's almost comical to experience the first time, because it's so surprising. When the plane stops and the bell sounds to notify the passengers that they can deplane (and often, before the bell sounds), people jump up into the aisles as if there is a fire, and shove their way to the front of the plane.

It doesn't matter if these individuals were seated in the first row or 15 rows back. If they can get ahead, they will do it. Usually, no consideration is given to whoever is seated in the rows they are passing. It seems to be a game of who can get off the plane first.

We've visited numerous other Latin countries, and have never seen anything like this. The lack of personal space here really comes into play when someone is breathing down your neck, trying to get around you. My husband and I have made our annoyance at this practice into a game in recent years to amuse ourselves in lieu of getting really annoyed. Now we get up, block the aisles where our seats are, and don't allow anyone to get around us. The offending passengers will eventually give up, but it may take them several minutes before they do so.

Navigating at the Supermarket

You know how when you're shopping for groceries and you encounter other carts in the aisles? One or the other of you moves aside and lets the other cart pass. That's common courtesy. Well, in Panama, that habit doesn't really exist. If there's a chance for someone else to get in front of you, they generally will. So, it's up to you to force your way out into the flow of things, in order to keep moving. Otherwise you may end up stuck in one place or another while others just keep moving around you. This will feel like you're being really rude at first. Again, you'll get used to it.

Front Row Seating

When I think of sitting in the front row anywhere, I always think of getting in trouble in school. No one ever wanted to sit in the front row, where I come from. Everyone normally sat at least three rows back, even for business conferences. Well, in Panama, everyone wants to sit in the front row. I was actually at the inauguration of a trade show once and a VIP friend invited me to sit with her in the front row. I did, even though I was not a VIP. But she had invited me, so I didn't think anything of it. Well, when some other actual VIPs showed up, I was asked to move! I found it funny, because I really did not care, but the other people did care and they wanted to be seen in the front row.

When I queried a Panamanian colleague about this, he told me, "Panamanians want to feel important; when they have the chance, they want to be seen. They clamor to sit in the front row, to be photographed, to be visible. That's how they equate importance." It's true. You'll also see this play out in the newspapers and magazines that include social pages with photos of local events. It's the *People* magazine phenomenon. Everyone wants to be famous.

Other Physical Realities

Bad Breath

With the lack of personal space, you'll smell a lot more bad breath. Get used to it. Dental hygiene is not as common in this country, because it's considered expensive for most people. In most companies, dental insurance is not offered as an option. The milk in Panama is treated differently. I'm not quite sure how – it certainly tastes fine – but the pasteurization or the homogenization processes are somehow different. My experience has been that milk products sour faster, and drinking a lot of milk products contributes greatly to bad breath here. Heavy coffee consumption is also a contributor, and of course, there's a lot of great coffee here.

Body Odor

Well, it is a tropical country. You sweat more. Others sweat more. Everyone smells more. Most locals are generally pretty generous with their cologne or perfume. Because the climate is so different from where they came from, most expats have a hard time determining how the heat and humidity impact their own bodily processes.

You're going to smell others more frequently, and you're going to smell yourself more than you ever have. Make whatever adjustments to your own personal hygiene to accommodate this factor.

Attire and Dress Code

Panama is much more formal than most other countries are. While you can read about this in a lot of other books, what's important to know is this: you cannot come here and wear your shorts and flip flops everywhere you go. In most government offices, in fact, you'll be turned away at the door and refused service if that's what you wearing.

This may feel extreme to you, at first. It did to us. What you'll find is that shorts (or, as Panamanians refer to them, *short pants*) are normally worn only on the weekends. Even when someone is out and about in public during the week in Panama, you'll see them in jeans, long pants, or a dress. It's as if the fringe of a more formal era when people dressed more properly is still hanging on.

Generally in Panama, the dress code is what I recall from the 1980's in the U.S. Not in terms of style, but in terms of formality. Most people actually dress up a bit here, even for their everyday round.

The Pretty Woman Syndrome

There's a beauty to this formality, especially when it comes to women. Women here like to look pretty. Panamanian women are meticulous about their hair and make-up, anytime they're in public. Even our housekeeper shows up to go to work in heels and lipstick. She takes off both before starting her daily tasks, but before she leaves, she takes 15 minutes to get pretty again.

This is a pretty big difference from the Gringo habit of running out the door looking like you've just gotten out of bed. (Granted, this is less prevalent among the Baby Boomer generation than it is in the younger millennial generation, but still.)

Ladies, you'll notice that women wear dresses here more frequently. When we moved here, I had maybe two dresses in my wardrobe. I never wore them in the U.S. You are in the tropics now, however, and with the climate, you'll find you stay cooler in a dress. My wardrobe now includes about 15 dresses. It's very appropriate to put on a dress to go to dinner – even a casual dinner – with friends. If you attend church, wear a dress.

Promiscuous Dress

No one can come to Panama and not immediately notice the marked difference in how women here dress. I'm talking about cleavage, camel-toe pants, skin-tight dresses, low-cut blouses, form fitting *everything*, and four to six inch high heeled shoes that are worn with every outfit imaginable! For a Latin country that is deemed so religious (70% Catholic), one might think that the way women dress here indicates they don't have any issues with their body image.

For newcomers, this visual parade of the female form can be stimulating (especially for men) and/or irritating (especially for women). Don't take it personally. Women in Latin America – not just in Panama – simply dress more provocatively than they do in other parts of the world. Their male Latin counterparts like it and encourage it, so it's not going to change. In my opinion, I've found that living surrounded by this culture has helped me loosen up a bit, and introduce some more revealing items into my normally staid wardrobe.

Because this sexy style is prevalent here, many women will show up at the office with cleavage and tight clothing in place, looking like they're heading out for a night on the town. If you object to this, it's important to establish a dress code that you feel is appropriate, and communicate it to your employees. Be sure to put it in writing too. Don't expect that common sense will rule in this type of issues, as the norms differ according to culture. What seems perfectly fine to a Panamanian may offend you, and vice versa.

Business Attire

In business, it's still very appropriate and standard for men to wear suits. Some offices are beginning to relax, but Panama is much more conservative in dress for business. The business casual culture of khaki pants and polo shirts has not made its way here yet. Some companies are beginning to embrace casual days on Fridays, but this is not yet widely accepted.

Gentlemen, plan to wear a business suit everywhere you go in Panama for business meetings. It's a way to ensure that you're seen as an equal by everyone you meet. Men of means and influence are expected to look a certain way.

Image is hugely important here. Yes, you can remove your jacket when you're eating lunch, when others in a business meeting do so, or you're in the car. Most of the time you'll be inside an office with air conditioning blasting, and you'll be comfortable.

As a general rule, ladies in business should take a look at what their counterparts in the office are wearing. This can be a guide for your own attire, but be certain to consider your female counterparts who have the same level of title that you do.

Other helpful tips for women in business include:

- If you're an executive, wear a suit, no matter what others around you are wearing.

- This commands respect from your male counterparts.
- If you have any doubt about what to wear, always wear a skirted suit.
- It's always better to dress up than to dress down.
- Heels can be and normally are worn with every outfit.
- Some type of jewelry is always worn. (Minimalism has not yet made it to Panama.)
- Not many women wear hosiery in Panama, unless they work in a bank, where it is required. Use your best judgment on this issue.
- Get or give yourself manicures on a regular basis. The Latin culture uses their hands very demonstratively when speaking, so more attention is given to the hands.
- Attractive high-heeled sandals are fine even for the office, as long as your toenails have had a recent pedicure.

Panama Hats

Gentlemen, please don't wear a Panama hat everywhere you go. People will think you are a tourist because tourists are the only ones who wear them. Save that for when you go back to your home country, and perhaps there someone will think its fun. Here, it's not. In fact, if you read history, the hat that is called the *Panama hat* actually comes from Ecuador. The true Panama hat is one that you'll see the farmers (locally called *campensinos*) wearing on the side of the road. It is turned up in the front and has a wider bill. Even so, most expats or Panamanians of means don't wear them.

Black Tie Affairs

Before we moved to Panama, I had not had a long formal dress in my wardrobe since college. Since we've been here, I've purchased three. Many evening events are true black tie events, where men are expected to wear a tuxedo (or at a minimum, a dark color, formal suit) and women wear long formal dresses.

If you get invited to a wedding or purchase a ticket to an evening event, check your invitation as to the requested attire for the evening. Ladies, a sundress for this type of event is definitely *not* appropriate; nor are khakis and open collared shirts for men. People take these events seriously, so it's important to dress as requested. If you have a question, it's better to dress up than to dress down.

At the Beach

At the beach on the weekends, pretty much anything goes. Being at the beach is all about relaxation, so t-shirts, shorts, sundresses, flip flops, swimsuits (with cover-ups), and casual attire are fine. If you're meeting friends out for dinner at a restaurant, plan to shower before you go and wear nice casual clothes, not your beachfront things. If you're staying at a hotel or resort, dinner attire should be nicer than what you had on when you came back from the pool.

Summary

Overall, the dress code is more formal in Panama. If you're visiting, you can get a good sense of this at restaurants, at the mall and by visiting places of business, like banks, schools or hospitals. This will give you a realistic view of how your own wardrobe might need to evolve when you live here.

11

HOLIDAYS

Holidays in Panama

PANAMA HAS 13 business holidays during the calendar year. The U.S. has six observed national holidays: New Year's Day, Memorial Day, July 4, Labor Day, Thanksgiving and Christmas. In Panama, **more than double** that amount are celebrated, including:

- New Year's Day, January 1
- Martyr's Day, January 9
- Carnival (February or March) – 3 days (the equivalent of Mardi Gras)
- Good Friday (Friday before Easter)
- Labor Day, May 1
- Independence from Colombia, November 3
- Flag Day, November 4
- Colon Independence Day (Colon is a city on the Atlantic side), November 5
- Independence from Spain, November 28
- Mother's Day, December 8
- Christmas Day, December 25

All of Panama's holidays fall between November 1 and May 1, with the bulk of them in the months of November,

December and February (assuming Carnaval falls in February, which it normally does).

The Impact of Holidays

If you own your own company or are managing a work team, it's important to know upfront what kind of impact the holiday schedule will have on your productivity during the year. Panamanians are very serious about their holidays, so you cannot expect anyone to work on a national day off. If, for some reason, you've asked someone to do so, they may tell you they will—but the likelihood of them actually showing up is slim to none. <u>It's better not to ask</u>.

Between late October and the end of December, you'll notice a big change in how things operate in the country overall. The Independence and Flag Days, which are celebrated November 3-5 every year, are the biggest holidays of the year for Panamanians – referred to as *Dias Patrias*. On this holiday more than half the city's inhabitants head for the Interior, (beach, family homes, whatever), with their families. Most locals will extend these three national holidays into a week, if they can. Add in the preparation (both physical and mental) and the excitement that goes with a week off with family, friends and national pride thrown in, and you'll see productivity in your office sharply decline, starting in the last week of October. If you're planning or scheduling anything important during the month of November, I recommend that you change it. Move the date to either October or January, because the normal schedules simply will not function as they do in other parts of the year. It's that serious.

In February, the *Carnavales* holidays happen. These are the second biggest holidays for Panamanians; so again, things come to a grinding halt. A lot of people go to the Interior, so traffic on the PanAmerican highway is heavy and slow. Like Dias Patrias, many Panamanians will turn these two to three days into a full week off.

In April, Easter is celebrated. But in this country, because of the prominence of Catholicism, you'll see many people in church every day of the week the full week before Easter Sunday. Good Friday is a national holiday too, and many people take the day before (Maundy Thursday) off or leave at noon.

My husband and I estimate that productivity decreases by 40% each year between late October and mid-February in the entire country. It's as if half the country mentally checks out in between all the holidays. Efficiency in this time period does not exist, and you'll find that people become less dependable than they usually are.

The first year we lived here, I did the Gringo thing. My body clock was not used to so many days off in November and December, so I worked through many of them. I was frustrated when my staff did not complete tasks and deadlines as previously agreed. I got mad. Tension grew in the office. It did not matter. Then, months later, when my U.S. holidays were not being observed in Panama (and my body clock was expecting them), I had to work. Then, I was mad at myself that I hadn't taken advantage of the holidays earlier. And it was my own damn fault.

Here's what I've learned: RELAX. You now live in Panama, so take the Panamanian holidays. Adopt the culture and enjoy it. It's all part of the laid back lifestyle you'll find here. Just don't expect much else to happen in the midst of all of them, because it won't. This applies to all business, including any day-to-day mundane stuff you might need to accomplish – anything at the bank, your utilities, any repairs, etc.

One Final Note About Holidays

For a few of them – January 9, Good Friday (in March or April, the Friday before Easter Sunday), and November 2nd – liquor sales are frozen for a period of 24 hours starting at 6 p.m. the night before the holiday starts through 6 p.m. on that day. So, mark your calendar and plan ahead if purchasing liquor is part of your celebration.

12

ROUGH EDGES

FOR ALL INTENTS and purposes, Panama is a developing nation. There are still a lot of aspects to this country that are unsophisticated. The beauty of Panama being a bit off the beaten path (or on the brink of discovery) is that you can still experience some amazing places that are largely untouched by civilization and development.

Some of the best places we've ever been in our lives are part of Panama's more rustic regions, such as the San Blas islands, where the Guna (formerly called Kuna) Indians rule on the Caribbean or Atlantic coast. Bocas Del Toro on the Caribbean side, close to Costa Rica, is stunningly beautiful, with snorkeling that looks like something out of a Technicolor movie. (Bocas Del Toro is where the *Survivor Panama* series was filmed.) Many other books and guides can give you recommendations on great destinations within the country to visit. Part of your opportunity as a new resident in Panama is the chance to do some reasonably priced travel within the country, as Panama's regions are very different from one to the other.

But as with anything in development, Panama still has a lot of rough edges.

There are many things here that are very similar to how they were in the U.S. in the 1960s or the 1970s. A lot of daily processes are just now, in 2012, being turned from paper to digital, and that means they generally take more time. In fact, it's best to count on spending <u>two to three times more time getting something accomplished here</u> than you would do in the U.S. Sometimes it's more than that.

The paragraphs below delve into some of the less polished aspects you'll find in the country. It helps to know what to expect.

Infrastructure

While it's improved over the past five years, and public works are now undergoing a massive renovation and rebuilding, infrastructure here still leaves a lot to be desired. Especially if you come from the U.S., where maintenance by the government happens on a regular basis.

Here, potholes may remain in place for months at a time, if they are ever fixed. In the metropolis of Panama, these things will be fixed faster than in the Interior. (Note: The word *Interior* is what the locals call the countryside, named for the interior of the isthmus, and encompassing anything West of the Panama Canal and not in the city of Panama.)

Over time, you'll figure out what streets to avoid, and how to get around the places where significant repair is needed. This helps, because tires here can be expensive.

Traffic congestion on the PanAmerican Highway

Traffic

In the recent past, Panama has been mentioned in some publications as one of the worst cities in the world for traffic. Some have said it's on par with Mumbai, India. In Panama, you will find that traffic is a big, disorganized mess. There are many more cars on the road than appropriate roadways for them, and the result is significant congestion. Somehow, the process of getting from one place to another eventually functions, but it's one of the biggest complaints you'll hear on a regular basis. And it's warranted.

Because Panama is currently under construction for a new metro bus and train system, it's made traffic in the city 30% worse than usual. This is short-term pain for long term gain as of this writing in late 2012, but it's going to take another two to three years to sort itself out. If the pace of growth continues in Panama and more people relocate here, it's hard to imagine that this will improve even at the end of the construction period. Only time will tell.

(Happily, you won't be fighting chickens, goats and cows for the road, unless you're deep in the countryside.)

Planning for Travel

No matter what, traffic will have a big impact on your day-to-day life in Panama. It takes a lot of time, and it's important to learn how to adjust your schedule to allow for traffic.

I like to describe driving in Panama as if one were a fish in a stream. Stop signs and stoplights do exist, as do many other types of signage. However, people pay little attention to them. What you'll notice is that traffic just flows, and there's little to no order about it. When someone wants to turn from the far left lane to take a right hand onto the next street, they might start leaning into your lane to do so. Or they might just cut you off. Normally, this will happen without the use of a turn signal.

If a car decides to merge into the lane you're in, it will often seem to almost drive into your car, in order to cut off the car behind you. Meaning, you'll look up and there will be three to four inches of space between your side door and their bumper. This can make the driving experience pretty stressful, especially for those of us used to orderly traffic systems.

Lane closures and road construction can be very challenging. These are often signaled poorly, with no notice. Although in the U.S., you'd see road construction well in advance with big orange signs and flashing lights, that's a rarity in Panama. A single cone or two may be placed immediately in front of a big hole, leaving you to take an immediate hard left or right. This can be harrowing, especially on a highway, when traveling at high speeds.

My husband likens driving in Panama to a video game, which is a great description. At any given moment, cars will cut you off, crowd you, pedestrians may appear out of nowhere, and lanes that were open the day before will suddenly be closed. You never know what the next moment will bring.

You may find it interesting that road rage does not exist in Panama. We've only seen it once. Bad manners in traffic are the norm, but no one gets excited or upset. You won't see a lot of angry faces behind windshields, arms waving out of windows, or bird gestures through windshields. For the most part, everyone seems to take the traffic and related congestion in stride.

Trash

The most common complaint I hear from expats and visitors alike is about trash. Panama is in desperate need of an anti-trash campaign by the government. However, one has not hit the market to date.

Most Panamanians have the same attitude about trash that existed in the U.S. until the 1960's and 70's…i.e….'Someone else will pick it up'. They don't consider it their problem, because a workforce of human street sweepers exists. (Machines have now taken on this duty in other countries.)

The bottom line is you'll see trash everywhere – in the city, in the country, and on the beach.

The purveying attitude locally can best be described by the following example: A friend of ours encountered several of his employees waiting for the bus, so he stopped to pick them up. As they climbed into his car, one of the gals said, *'Wow, your car is so dirty, let me help you clean it up.'* She then subsequently started throwing napkins and fast food bags out the window! My friend said *'Wait! Don't do that! You're making my trash someone else's problem.'* Truly, this was an educational moment for the local gal, who was surprised by his reaction.

Unfortunately, this is the norm. Until recently, you could scarcely locate a public trashcan to dispose of anything in a public park, on the street corner or outside a place of business. Happily, that is starting to change.

Roadside Urination

A large portion of the male population in Panama doesn't hold back when they need to urinate. As a result, the rest of the traveling public gets to view them (or sometimes several of them simultaneously) relieving themselves on the side of the road. Again, unfortunately, this is something you'll see in all areas of the country – urban and rural.

Pay Day

People's paycheck schedules in Panama have a huge impact on traffic. Approximately 30% of the population works for the government. Government workers get paid on the 14th and the 28th of each month. Non-government workers get paid on the 15th and the 30th of each month. That means that all workers on those dates have money to fill up their gas tanks and do all of their semi-weekly errands.

You'll notice on Pay Days that the streets suddenly have double the amount of cars, lines at the banks and the markets are longer, and traffic is a huge mess. We didn't personally believe this phenomenon when we first heard about it. But now, we plan for it. We literally look at the calendar to see when Pay Days fall within the month, and avoid those days for errands (or meetings) as much as possible. Believe me, once you experience it for yourself, you'll do the same.

Decimo (or Special Pay Days)

The labor law in Panama calls for three Special Pay Days per year. These are called Decimo. It's when a worker receives one-third of their monthly salary, as a bonus. Every Panamanian worker is due this every year, according to the law. These *Decimo* payments fall on April 15, August 15 and December 15. On these dates, it's best to plan to stay at home or in your office the entire day, as the resulting traffic is worse than any other time of the year (except for December).

December and Christmas time

During the month of December, the city is almost brought to its knees by traffic. Here's why:

- There are two big holidays – December 8th (Mother's Day) and December 25th (Christmas Day)
- *Decimo* falls on December 15th
- Holiday shopping
- Holiday parties and family get-togethers

The short story is to drive as little as possible during the month of December, especially during evening hours and on weekends. If you receive invitations for, and plan to attend holiday gatherings, plan for your travel to take two to three times longer in traffic.

Getting a Driver

Because the traffic experience can be such a culture shock, I strongly recommend that expats new to Panama consider hiring a driver. Why? Keep reading.

A driver can be hired full-time in Panama for about $500-600 per month (not including benefits, like social security). For the amount of time it can take to get from one place to another in Panama, it's well worth the cost. We hired one when we first came to town, and five years later, he's still with us. He's been worth every cent we've paid him, because of the following:

- He knows all the back routes that no one else knows which has saved us countless hours of travel.
- Having a driver helped us learn the city streets, directions and one way street system. (Panama is not laid out on a grid, so it takes almost a year to figure out where things are and how to find them. There are few street signs, and many buildings do not have good signage or numbering. Having a driver helps negate all of this.)
- In the early months, it eliminated the stress of learning to drive ourselves in the country out of the picture. Instead, we could concentrate on the business at hand.

- There's never sufficient parking in the city. With a driver, you can be dropped off and picked up at the door of wherever you're going, instead of circling the area for an hour looking for a parking place.
- It's been a huge time saver in terms of errands. Because Panama still has many non-automated processes, a driver can also do many time-consuming things for you, such as:
  - Stand in line to pay your bills.
  - Pick up documents from your attorney, insurance company, or the government.
  - Help you get your car license plates done.
  - Pick up items for you from the supermarket or pharmacy.
  - Walk your dog.
  - Take and drop clothing off at the dry cleaner.
  - And the list goes on.

Utilities

Panama has very consistent utility service, except after big rains or storms. We've found it's a good idea to have a two to three day backup supply of drinking water stored in your pantry. In a worst-case scenario, you can use the water to take a sponge bath, if needed.

In early 2012, parts of Panama City's water system were out of commission for up to six days. People had to get creative as to their daily routine, as you can imagine. (Not to mention their sanitary habits.) The best advice is to get that backup supply of water and keep it in your pantry. If you never have to use it, that's great. But if the water goes out, and you don't have it… well, don't say you weren't warned.

Electricity costs are very high in Panama. You can expect to pay at least double or triple what you did in the U.S.

Cell phone service in Panama is relatively good. There are now four providers. At this writing, Claro provides the best coverage in the country, in my opinion. (Note: this is not a promotion or a recommendation for Claro; this is based on my own experience). That said, do your homework and ask others for their recommendations.

Panama claims that it has the best telecom connectivity in the Americas, second to New York City, which seems a bit farfetched. However, for the majority of the country, wireless coverage for your smart phone is accessible for the most part, so perhaps there's some validity to that statement. Coverage is non-existent or spotty at best in more remote places like San Blas and the Darien.

Emergency Services

Police

The national police just started using cars on the streets in 2011. That may sound pretty strange, but it's true. As recently as 2010, patrol policeman were dropped off on street corners every day. If they wanted to stop you for a traffic infraction, they'd simply walk in front of your car. It wasn't necessarily safe, but it worked.

Today, the police have a proper fleet of cars. They're white vehicles, with the usual sirens and lights on top. This means they can now chase bad guys, if needed. It's a big improvement. No one really took the police that seriously when they were just hanging out on street corners.

In the 50's and 60's in places like Chicago, you could easily bribe the police when they stopped you in lieu of giving you a ticket. That practice in Panama was still pretty prevalent as late as 2010. That seems to be less the case in recent years, which is comforting. There's also a rise in the number of women police officers in the last two years, and they don't seem to let things slide like some of their male counterparts did.

It is a visual affront to most North Americans when they first arrive in Panama to see policemen in combat attire. Combat attire here looks like the attire worn in many militaries. They wear green fatigues, with black boots, helmets and bulletproof vests. They carry machine guns or rifles. Of course, this is nothing like police forces in many other places, so for some, it's a bit intimidating at first.

Don't worry. You'll get used to it. Most of the time, these are the police assigned to high-traffic areas, or areas that historically are called 'red zones'. It's a good idea to avoid the red zones at night, as they have a higher incidence of crime.

Otherwise, you will see these combat police occasionally appear in your neck of the woods. Usually that means a high-ranking government official or the country's president is visiting or speaking at an event close-by.

Combat police are a regular presence in Casco Viejo – the old city – where the president's offices are located.

Minor incidents and traffic tickets

Panama law requires that an incident report form be carried in every car in Panama. This form is required to be filled out, if you have an accident. These days with smart phones, it's also easy to take good photos, which come in handy for filing insurance. The law does require that you and the other party move your cars out of traffic, unless there's a major injury. Then, you wait for your insurance carrier and the police to arrive to file the report. (You'll probably be there for a while, so it's a good idea to carry snacks and water in your car at all times. No joke.)

If you ever have an issue, don't expect a lot of help from the police. Here's an example why.

We were returning from the beach to the city one Sunday. On a narrow, country road, another car ran us off the road and caused damage to our car. We stopped to speak to the other driver, who became violent. Others witnessed the incident, and the police were called. Forty-five minutes later, they came, but the offending driver had fled the scene.

The attending officer took down our version of the incident, and then proceeded to go look for the other driver. Of course, he didn't find him in the near vicinity. Having nothing more to go on besides our description, there was not much that could be done. We were asked to go to the nearby police station to file a report. We thought that was what we had done when we gave the policeman that came to the scene the story, but apparently it was not enough. (You'll discover that in Panama, if a *report* is mentioned, it's an indication that a document must be typed up on a formal, triplicate form by someone who sits behind a desk.)

When we arrived at the local police station, we were asked to wait. After 20 minutes, the chief came out and told us there really was not much they could do to help us. No further report was written up, and our car damage was our own problem.

This was maddening, but it taught us a good lesson. When you are down here, you're pretty much on your own. If you know this fact coming in, then you won't be surprised if this happens to you. And, best of all, you can be prepared (at least mentally).

Litigation and Personal Responsibility

Panama is not a litigious society. There aren't attorneys waiting in the wings to sue you for every little thing at the drop of a hat. In many ways, this is very refreshing. It means people have to take personal responsibility.

If your kid climbs a wall that does not have a fence around it, it's your responsibility to tell your kid not to climb on the wall. If the restaurant pours you a hot cup of coffee, it's your responsibility to test it first, before you drink it. It's your problem if you burn your mouth, or if your kid falls and breaks his arm. There's simply no one else to blame.

I personally like this. I tire of the idea that someone can 'take everything you own' just because they're not happy with you in the U.S.

So, the good news is, you've just stepped back about 50 years. Yes, there are some lawsuits, but they are few and far between, at least to date.

Conducting Legal Business

If you have legal business to conduct in any fashion, expect that it will take much, much longer from start to finish. Anyone who moves to Panama should locate and hire a good local attorney. Most cultures don't really have a family attorney anymore, as most legal business can be conducted personally or online.

That's not the case here in Panama. 99% of any type of legal action must involve a local Panamanian attorney. So, one of the things you need to do here (soon after you relocate) is find and hire a good attorney.

The good news is that there are plenty of attorneys in the country. The bad news is you have to figure out who will best service you and your needs. Like any other important decision, do your homework. Get online, check out the company's website, and then get references from other expats. Meet with a number of attorneys and ask each for their own references.

The relationship you will build with your attorney is key to your legal protection and success in Panama for all of your business transactions, so it's important you locate one you feel very comfortable with.

Skyscrapers and slums in Panama City

Social Norms

When growing up, we used to refer to certain states in the U.S. - like Mississippi or West Virginia – as backward. Meaning the people there were less educated, or less socially polished. Most of the time it was a joke; of course. But, there's something to be said for a place that has lower levels of education, and thus, less sophisticated social norms. Here are some examples of how that rings true in Panama.

Bad News

Most North Americans don't have an issue addressing a problem. Especially if that problem was caused by someone else. In fact, North Americans often start a discussion about a problem that can quickly lead to a confrontation. Panamanians avoid confrontation like the plague. We call it the bad news syndrome.

If there's bad news of any kind that needs to be delivered, you'll rarely hear it in Panama. Here are some examples of how that frequently happens, so that you know what to look for along the way. It's important to know these, as most newly relocated expats have no idea that this phenomenon exists, and it can be a huge surprise. (Unfortunately, the surprise is too often at their expense, or to their detriment.)

- If someone is not going to keep an appointment they have with you, not only will they often *not show up*, they *may not call you to cancel* either.
- You may receive a phone call to confirm an appointment, as late as 30 minutes before the appointment is scheduled to start. (This baffled me at first, but in many ways, it's a courtesy to you, given the prevalence of people not showing up for appointments here.)
- If the work you ordered (with a contractor or a vendor) is going to be delayed, the person doing the work will stop answering their phone when you call to check on the status.
- The contractor or vendor will eventually get back to you, but it will be when <u>they</u> are ready to give you an update on the status of the project, not necessarily when you are ready.
- If someone has made a mistake or wronged you, don't expect an apology.
- It's *highly* unlikely you'll ever hear an admission of wrongdoing in this country. Panamanians are a very proud people, and they don't like to look bad, even if they were the cause of something.
- When there's bad news, the cultural norm is that you won't hear *anything* about the topic at all, until it's too late. Think of yourself as a detective. If you feel like a topic is being avoided, it more than likely is. That

should be a red flag to you to start asking some questions. More often than not, if something has occurred that requires an explanation, you'll have to figure out for yourself what happened. Everyone else will avoid the topic like the plague.

- The phrase *'don't worry'* is overused in Panama. When you hear it repeatedly, you should typically start worrying. Or you can simply know that whatever you're inquiring about will be definitely be wrong, delayed or not come at all.

- When any of these situations happen to you, don't think of yelling at the person when you feel frustrated. When you yell or raise your voice at a Panamanian, it only backfires on you. The person will shut down, and you'll get nothing at all. So, keep your temper in check. Be as nice as you can, and then go home and punch your punching bag.

Here's the lesson: *When you know that avoiding bad news is a norm here, you can learn how to get around it.*

In my office, I trained my local staff by telling them this: *The sooner I know bad news, the better! It will help me find a solution, versus having one thing lead to another to make the problem bigger than it is. This will make it easier and faster for all of us. I need your help!*

Panamanians like to feel important, as do we all. So approach any delicate situation as if they are helping *you*, and you'll all come out feeling good about the process. (Note that this referenced coaching technique is only *now* presenting results after several years, and these are highly-qualified professionals.)

Generally, the less educated a person is, the more likely bad news will be avoided at all costs. (Go back to the earlier reference about the mentality of people who have been told what to do for centuries in Chapter 2). When people have been oppressed for generations, they aren't likely to speak up. They couldn't do so without facing severe punishment, or having to face confrontation, which is very uncomfortable for the local culture.

Whether it's your server, your housekeeper, your driver, or a clerk at the supermarket, the natural tendency here is that you just won't hear bad news. Or when you ask about something that's happened, you'll get a blank stare in return.

Helpful Tip:

When you feel like you are missing something, your hunch is probably right. So, it's up to you to figure out how to ask the right questions. Think of it like a treasure hunt!

Sexism and Sexual Harassment

Sexism is prevalent in Panama. Some examples:

- The glass ceiling for women still exists in Panama. In 2012, I can count on one hand the number of high-level Panamanian female executives that I know in this country. Most of the time, women are relegated to middle management and not much more, unless they are entrepreneurs. This is starting to change, thank

God, but it's endemic of the machismo that continues to thrive in Latin America.

- Motels, referred to as *push buttons* or *ding-dongs*, cater specifically to people having an illicit affair. They're designed so you can drive in, push a button, pay the fee, and depart without ever having come face-to-face with a motel clerk.
- Provocative attire is acceptable and encouraged, even at very young ages for girls.
- Whistling at women here is considered a compliment – in the States, it is considered extremely insulting and sexual harassment.
- In the upper class, a standard gift for a girl's coming of age party (Quincenera, when she turns 15) is a boob job. This is not a joke.
- Many Latin men think nothing of openly staring or leering at a woman's body. (*I've found the best way to counteract this is to look straight at the person, look them up and down in the same manner with a look of disapproval or disdain, and then, walk away. It gets the point across.*)
- Prostitution is still legal here.

Racism

Racism exists and it's prevalent. There are six different races in Panama, according to the national census. The darker your skin is, the less likely you are – if you are Panamanian – to enjoy the same opportunities as those with lighter skin. Those of black, Caribbean or Indian descent here are especially prone to having lower levels of education, fewer opportunities for developing themselves in a profession, and higher levels of racial discrimination.

We assumed when we moved here from North America that we'd enjoy living in a place where racism was less prevalent. We thought there'd be more tolerance, because everyone had a skin tone, from Spanish to black. Unfortunately, that's not the case. In fact, racism in Panama is ten times worse than it is in the U.S., and it's much more overt. Those with darker skin are normally relegated to be maids, drivers or administrative help.

As a result, it's socially acceptable to refer to someone by their race or their skin color – i.e. 'the black girl over there,' or 'the Chinese guy.' It's not considered denigrating to describe someone in that fashion.

Gays and Lesbians

If you're gay or lesbian and thinking of moving to Panama, my best advice is to choose another country. Panama is not very tolerant or accepting of the gay lifestyle, especially for anyone aged 40 or older. We've personally witnessed tolerance becoming less of a social issue than it was five years ago, but it's a slow process.

Recall that Panama is 70% Catholic (whether or not they're practicing), and most of them openly do not believe its okay to be gay. It's sad to report that we've personally witnessed widespread, open discrimination against gays in this country.

THE FINALE

THE TOP TEN LIST

Where else can you find untouched beauty like this?

THOSE OF US from the U.S. have seen David Letterman's top ten lists over the years, right? I love those. So, here's a list to take with you.

Your Top Ten Survival Tips for an Easier Time of it in Panama

1. Come to Panama, and spend at least a month here before you commit to moving here. If you have the flexibility, come down and sign a short-term lease (six months to a year) and try it out.

2. Write down your expectations and all the reasons why you are moving to Panama. Put them down on paper. Then re-read this book.

   a. Are your expectations and reasons realistic?

   b. Are you really up to the challenge? This is not a small thing you are doing. Moving is often ranked in the Top Three Most Stressful Events in one's life. On top of that...well, you've read the book.

   c. Make sure you are as mentally and emotionally prepared as possible, and adopt a realistic outlook. That's your best chance for success.

3. Locate and hire a good English-speaking attorney in Panama soon after you move.

   a. Ask everyone you know for a recommendation on this, and ask what that person uses the attorney for.

   b. Go meet two to three of those recommended, to get a personal feel for them, and to make sure you understand each other. Just because the person speaks English doesn't mean they will understand you.

4. Rent a home for at least six months in any neighborhood before you ever elect to purchase there.

5. Purchase the Rosetta Stone software to learn Spanish (if you've never had any classes).

    a. If you are more advanced, but need help conversationally, hire a tutor to come to your home once or twice a week.

    b. Stick with whatever language program you've chosen for at least two years.

6. Hire a full-time driver and employ him or her for the first full year (or two) that you live in Panama. (Cab drivers are especially useful, as they know all the short cuts.)

    a. This will allow you to figure out how to find your way around.

    b. The driver can help you with a lot of other tasks related to getting your life set up in Panama.

    c. How will you find one? Ask everyone you meet if they know of a reputable person looking for a driver job. If you meet a cab driver you like, ask him. Be sure to get references from anyone you interview and check them. Then do a background check.

    d. This investment will save you significant time, money and frustration in the long run.

7. Get out every week to socialize and make new expat friends. You're going to need the support.

8. Find a church, a community group, an association or a local bar to create your social network. Attend it at least once a month, if not more often.

9. Take regular get-away trips – within Panama – as often as you can. It will help you expand your horizons and appreciate all the beauty Panama has to offer you.

10. Within your first two years of full-time life in Panama, return to the U.S. at least twice a year.

    a. This will give you much-needed relief from your adaptation process, including being back among English speakers when the Spanish just gets to be too much.

    b. If you can afford it, I recommend leaving the country every three months.

A tour given by the Embera Indians on the Chagres River

Personal Summary

THERE ISN'T ONE, easy phrase to describe the experience our move to Panama has been. You've likely gotten a good picture of that, as you've read this book.

Panama is in and of itself a complex little country, with intersecting influences from around the world and a complicated history. At any crossroads geographically, you'll find a mix of cultures and ideas that have merged over time as people came, went and left their mark. That's the case in Panama.

A relatively quiet little country until the last 25 years, Panama is now booming with business and attracting people from all over the globe. This is naturally impacting the way things are done here, both good and bad. We've seen a lot of changes in the short time we've been here. What's described in these pages will undoubtedly evolve and change in the next five years. But some things – like culture and habits – will likely remain the same.

The diablo rojo is the outgoing bus system in Panama: known for its crazy colorful designs. Each one is unique.

Here's What I've Learned From the Past Five Years Here:

- I've learned just how good we really have it in the U.S.A. I really had no idea before.
- I've learned to appreciate wide streets, organized traffic, and the existence of safe sidewalks and street lighting.
- I've learned how to drive like a Panamanian. Sometimes this gets me into trouble when I go back to the States.
- I've learned how to be more grateful for family and friendships back home, because our time with them is so limited.
- I've learned to appreciate people we've met for who they are. We've made some pretty unlikely friends here, and they've expanded our outlook and our point of view.
- I've learned how to find common points of interest with new friends very quickly.

- I've learned to get over my uptight expectations about deadlines.
- I've learned to relax more.
- I've learned to feel a little sad that this is the last year of the Diablo Rojo – the old public bus system being phased out this year decorated individually in loud, raucous designs by their owners.
- I've learned to like eating fish.
- I've learned to snorkel without hyperventilating.
- I've learned how to be more self-sufficient (even though I thought I was before, it's expanded a lot here).
- I've learned how to tell when a Papaya is truly ripe.
- I've learned to be more open with my local girlfriends, asking for help when I need it.
- I've learned how to ask the right questions to get to the truth (i.e. bad news).
- I've learned how to give up my frustration when something's not going my way, and to figure out a way to have some fun with the situation.
- I've learned how to just let it go when all of the figuring and scheming does not work.
- I've learned to drink a lot more beer.
- I've learned to appreciate the simplicity of having fewer choices at the supermarket and the drug store. Now when we go back to the U.S., I get a little overwhelmed by 50 choices for toothpaste alone!

- I've learned to celebrate the moments (not days, not hours) when everything goes just as I planned – the first time.
- I've learned to cry more.
- I've learned how to use Skype.
- I've learned how to text my friends in the U.S. (and have them text me) for free.
- I've learned how to talk on the phone in Spanish – one of the hardest milestones in language learning.
- I've learned how to dress a little more sexily.
- I've learned how to dance salsa.
- I've learned how to play the part of the dumb Gringo when needed.
- I've learned how to surf, paddleboard and boogie board.
- I've learned to communicate in hand motions and Spanglish, when the right vocabulary in Spanish cannot be found.
- I've learned how to get used to sweating, almost all the time.
- I've learned to look for the beauty in the little things, every day. That perfect tomato. The flawless service at the coffee counter. The sole Pelican floating in the ocean. The moonlight coming through the clouds. The perfect wave. The smile my husband and I share when we discover some bad news.

We've grown exponentially as human beings since we've lived in Panama. I hope your experience here will be as hilarious, fruitful and as blessed as ours has been, and that the things shared here will help you along your journey to be more educated, wiser and more patient with yourself and others.

ABOUT THE AUTHOR

Elizabeth Vance is a future New York Times bestselling author in the making, as well as a business executive and speaker. She holds a degree in business from a well-known U.S. university, and has worked in banking, government, real estate, nonprofit and telecommunications for the past 20 years.

Elizabeth began writing as a hobby in mid 2011, and her first book is the **Gringo Guide to Panama**. Currently at work on her next two books, Vance lives in the Republic of Panama with her husband and their two daughters.

To learn more, visit www.PanamaGringoGuide.com

Follow Elizabeth Vance on Twitter - @panamagguide

Follow The Gringo Guide to Panama on Google +
https://plus.google.com/u/0/118297979809700611966/about